THE SECRETS OF SOCIAL MEDIA MARKETING

Learn step by step secrets on how the professionals use social media marketing to increase sales, make new customers and retain the ones they have in this book

ABOUT THE AUTHOR

Stephen Akintayo, an inspirational speaker and Serial Entrepreneur is currently the Chief Executive Officer of Stephen Akintayo Consulting International and Gtext Media and Investment Limited, a leading firm in Nigeria whose services span from digital marketing, website design, bulk sms, online advertising, Media, e-commerce, real estate, Consulting and a host of other services.

Born In Gonge Area of Maiduguri, Borno State. North Eastern part of Nigeria in a very poverish environment and with a civil Servant as a Mother who raise him and his four other siblings with her mega salary since his father's Contract Business had crumbled. Some of his passion for philanthropy was birthed by his humble Beginning.

In his word; "My Surname was poverty. Hunger was my biggest challenge. I had to scavenge all through Primary school to eat lunch as I don't go to school with lunch packs. We were too poor to afford that. Things got better in my secondary school days, though My mum will still go to her colleague to borrow money to send me to school each term.

It was humiliating seeing their disdain faces looking at my mum like a foolish woman who keeps begging. It hurts dearly. I hate Poverty and I pray to help more families come out of it".

Stephen Akintayo story is indeed a grass to grace one. His singular regret in life is that his hard working mother died few year back due to ovarian cancer and never lived to see some of the good works God is using him to do today.

Stephen, Also Founded GileadBalm Group Services which has assisted a number of businesses in Nigeria to move to enviable levels by helping them reach their clients through its enormous nationwide data base of real phone numbers and email addresses. It has hundreds of organizations as its clients including multinational companies like Guarantee Trust Bank, PZ Cussons, MTN,Chivita, among others.

He is also the Founder and President of Infinity Foundation and Stephen Akintayo Foundation, an indigenous non-governmental organization that assists orphans and vulnerable children as well as mentor young minds.

The foundation has assisted over 2,000 orphans and vulnerable children and has also partnered with 22 orphanage homes in the country. By December 2015 Infinity Foundation is starting Mercy Orphanage to care for victims of Boko haram attacks in the Northern part of Nigeria.

Stephen Akintayo Foundation focus on Financial Grants with Initial grant of 10,000,000 to 20 entrepreneur in 2015 plan to grow that to 500Million annual grant by the 5th year. Projects like Upgrade Conference and The Serial Entrepreneur Conference with thousands of attendee who benefit from the high value knowledge from exceptional speakers and consultants.

Stephen, popularly called Pastor Stephen is also the founder of Omonaija, an online radio station in Lagos currently streaming for 24 hours daily with the capacity to reach every country of the world.

He is the founder and Director of Digital Marketing School Nigeria. Africa's leading Digital Marketing school issuing diploma certificates with robust training curriculum in Digital Maketing,Tele Marketing and Neuro Marketing.

He is an Author of several published books including Turning Your Mess To Message, Soul Mate, Survival Instincts and Mobile Millionaire Stephen is a media personality in the Television, Radio and Print media. He is currently anchoring a programme on Radio Continental, tagged CEO Mentorship with Stephen Akintayo, and A TV Show coming airing in the last quarter of 2015 as well as currently running a weekly column in some of Nigeria's national papers, including The Nation Newspaper and The Union
Newspapers. He is also a social media guru.

His mentorship platform has helped thousands of people including graduates and undergraduates in the area of business as well as in relationships.

Stephen strongly believes young Nigerians with the passion for entrepreneurship can cause a business revolution in Nigeria and the world at large.

Stephen Akintayo is currently running Masters In Digital Marketing and MBA in Netherlands.

He is a trained Digital Marketing Consultant by the Digital Marketing Institute and Harvard University. He is also a trained Coach by The Coaching Academy UK. He has several other professional training inside and outside Nigeria.

He is First Degree is in Microbiology from Olabisi Onabanjo University, a member of Institute of Strategic Management. He is an ordained Pastor with Living Faith Church Worldwide and he is happily married and blessed with Two Sons; Divine Surprises and Future.

To invite Stephen Akintayo for a speaking engagement kindly email: invite@stephenakintayo.com or call:08188220066.

Copyright 2016
<u>IMPORTANT LEGAL STUFF</u>

This book is © Mr. Stephen Akintayo. All Rights Reserved. You may not sell this book, give it away, display it publicly, nor may you distribute it in any form whatsoever.

While reasonable attempts have been made to ensure the accuracy of the information provided in this publication, the author does not assume any responsibility for errors, omissions or contrary interpretation of this information and any damages or costs incurred by that.

This book is not intended for use as a source of legal, business, accounting or financial advice. All readers are advised to seek the services of competent professionals in legal, business, accounting and finance fields.

While examples of past results may be used occasionally in this work, they are intended to be for purposes of example only. No representation is made or implied that the reader will do as well from using any of the techniques mentioned in this book.

The contents of this book are based solely on the personal experiences of the author. The author does not assume any responsibility or liability whatsoever for what you choose to do with this information. Use your own judgment.

Any perceived slight of specific people or organizations, and any resemblance to characters living, dead or otherwise, real or fictitious, is purely unintentional. You are encouraged to print this book for easy reading. However, you use this information at your own risk.

TABLE OF CONTENT

1. About the Author ……………….Pg.3
2. Important Legal Stuff…………….Pg.5
3. Table of Content……………………Pg.6
4. Introduction to Social Media…Pg.7
5. Types of Social Media Platforms and Tools Used for marketing….Pg.   15
6. How to Create Social Media Campaign That Work……Pg.   33
7. Benefits of Adding Visual Contents to Your Campaigns on Social Media 36
8. Tips From Social Media Marketing Geniuses……………….Pg.   45
9. Characteristics of a Successful Social Media Campaign……Pg.   49
10. Strategies for Engaging the Social Media as a Marketing Tool…..Pg.   55

CHAPTER ONE
INTRODUCTION TO SOCIAL MEDIA MARKETING

INTRODUCTION TO SOCIAL MEDIA

Social media marketing has been known as one of the proven marketing strategies for some time now. This is why it is very important that as an entrepreneur, you utilize it to your advantage in order to Increase your brand recognition.

Social media is a powerful tool for business, both on and offline. Whether you're new to Internet marketing, or you're new and want to acquire knowledge on how to leverage social media to promote your business, then you are reading the right book.

All over the world, over 3 billion people log on to various social media networks daily searching for one thing or the other which means that the internet is so vast that you need to utilize it to your advantage.

With social media, you can easily draw potential customers give them the access to get in touch with you through. In addition, the use of social media platforms allows you to become more recognizable both to your existing customers and their personal contacts too, provided you are smart enough to get them to share or repost your content.

WHAT IS SOCIAL MEDIA MARKETING

Social Media Marketing is the process of gaining website traffic or visitors through social media sites. Social media marketing campaigns usually center on efforts to create content that attracts attention and encourages readers to share them across their own social networks to their contacts.

REASONS WHY SOCIAL MEDIA MARKETING IS IMPORTANT

Social media marketing is a very important means every online entrepreneur must utilize to their full advantage. The benefits of social media marketing includes:

1. BRAND RECOGNITION

The internet is so large that you have to seize every opportunity you can to improve your brand recognition. Since social media networks are widely used these days all over the globe, using it to your advantage is a must. It can serve as a voice for your brand which can help you build your reputation and visibility. Through social media, an entrepreneur can attract potential customers and it will be a lot easier for them to get in touch with them through this medium. Also, using social media platforms allows you to become more recognizable not only to your existing customers but to their personal contacts too, if they share or repost your content.

2. BETTER OPPORTUNITIES

Social media marketing also provides you with better opportunities in terms of converting potential customers to buying clients. Social media allows you to connect with an infinite web of relationships through your followers, existing contacts and target audience. By posting a video, a link to a blog, a campaign or perhaps a simple photo related to your business or any topic relevant to your company, you will be able to spark a reaction. Each of these reactions obtained from a single post is a chance for a possible conversion.

3. INCREASED TRAFFIC AND CONVERSION RATES

If you use social media marketing the right way, you can tremendously increase your website traffic and even your conversion rates. All this is made possible by social media because it promotes interaction between 2 individuals or a group. This makes marketing more efficient because of the addition of interaction between multiple human beings. Inbound traffic to your site is greatly increased as well since you will no longer be limited to potential customers belonging to your personal contacts and existing customers.

If you use the right social media marketing strategies, you'll be able to attract the existing members of your niche or followers in a specific social media platform that you've selected. This also gives you better chances of increasing your sales potential.

If you are not yet into social media marketing, you better start as soon as you can because the longer you wait the more opportunities you are missing.

4. EXPAND YOUR REACH AND SPY ON YOUR COMPETITION

Apart from the benefit of engagement and building better relationships with your customers, you will also get to expand your reach without having to force your brand to your target audience. Commenting on live events creates content that is much more likely to be shared and hence go viral.

By following your competition, you can see what kind of deals they are offering customers, and keep up to date with other things they have going on. Just be sure that whatever you have to offer is better

Examples of tools you can use to achieve this include SEObook, marketing trader, Topsy, Google alerts, SEMRush, SpyFu etc

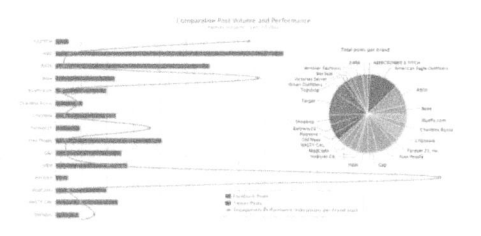

5. BUILDING RELATIONSHIPS

Real time social media marketing will also pave the way for you to build relationships with your audience. This is probably one of the best things that you can get from this kind of strategy. You'll get to engage with your followers in a real time conversation which is very important if you wish to build on the trust of your customers and reputation of your brand.

Social media also allows you to build and enhance both personal and professional relationships. You can use it to connect with other industry experts, or find old friends from high school you're looking to reconnect with

6. ESTABLISHING A BRAND AND RAISING AWARENESS

The majority of people on the Internet today are using at least one social media network, such as Facebook, Twitter, or Google+.

A good bit of them are using two, or even all three of those social networks. Getting your brand out there on those platforms is a good way to let people know you are around.

CHAPTER TWO
TYPES OF SOCIAL MEDIA PLATFORMS AND TOOLS USED FOR MARKETING

TYPES OF SOCIAL MEDIA PLATFORMS AND TOOLS USED FOR MARKETING

A social media platform is a web-based technology which enables the development, deployment and management of social media solutions and services. It provides the ability to create social media websites and services with complete social media network functionality.

TYPES OF SOCIAL MEDIA PLATFORMS

There are various social media platforms and tools experts use to promote their businesses online, advertise their goods and services and engage their customers.

Some of these platforms include twitter, Instagram, Facebook, google+, LinkedIn, blog, Tumblr, YouTube, Pinterest. Examples of social media tools include Hootsuite, Buffer, Ninja blaster and many more.

1. TWITTER

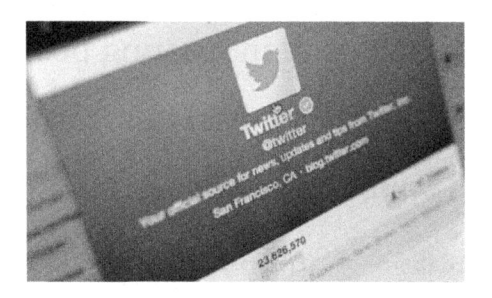

Quite similar to Facebook, Twitter has its own unique branding and a nice way of social interaction. It's the ultimate social network when it comes to viral content. Twitter had been home to the ever popular "hashtag" which has become a worldwide trend when it comes to posting catchy and interesting posts. The addition of celebrity users has also made twitter a handy form of entertainment. Twitter also has massive amounts of users which makes it a target for social media marketing

BENEFITS OF USING TWITTER FOR SOCIAL MEDIA MARKETING

RESEARCH

With the use of hashtags making it easy to research nearly any topic imaginable, the built in search feature is a valuable research tool. While the functionality will not replace the competitive research tools out there on the market today, it can help gather information about what's hot in the market, and where needs are within a particular niche.

DRIVE TRAFFIC TO YOUR WEBSITE

Many people will tweet their new blog posts out to their followers. However, just tweeting about your new blog post doesn't mean people will listen and click.

For this to work, you need to be actively involved in the network, and sharing valuable information your network is interested in or is looking for.

ENGAGE WITH CUSTOMERS

Businesses can communicate with their customer base, and get feedback in a causal, and cost effective way. Find out what your customers love (or hate) about what you have to offer, and make changes to improve it for them.

NETWORKING

Twitter enables you to connect and communicate with friends and family, but it can also be a powerful professional networking tool. In addition, it can be a great way for employees within the same organization to communicate back and forth because it is so short and to the point.

BRANDING

Matching your Twitter handle to your business name, and using custom graphics on your Twitter profile can be a great way to reinforce your brand, and to help raise awareness in its early stages.

How to Get Followers on Twitter

Make sure what you post has value. People will ignore you if it's garbage.

- **Use hashtags.** This categorizes what you're talking about, which makes it easier for people to find.

- **Tweet on topic most of the time.** At least 80% of the time, talk about your business niche. This helps establish your credibility.

- **Make use of your profile space.** Describe who you are, and link to your website.
- **Link to your profile from other social media profiles.** This helps people see that you are on Twitter.
- **Include your Twitter link in your email signature.** This too, helps people see that you are on Twitter.

- **Advertise your twitter link on your business cards.** This helps with offline marketing efforts and may bring additional followers.

- **Use Twitter search.** Find people who you want to connect with. See who's talking about what, and jump in the conversation.

- **Use @s.** @twitterhandle lets you engage a person directly. Do this often!

- **Use Follow Friday (#FF)** Not only will this help you suggest other people to your followers, you may find some awesome new connections this way.

- **Follow Friends of Friends.** This can help you find other relevant followers to engage.

Making Tweets

- **Use a URL shortener.** Something like bit.ly or owl.ly will shorten your URL to save you characters in your tweet, and it'll help you track the number of times it was clicked.
- **Share information of value.** Whether it's yours or not, share something you think your followers can use. You'll get more respect when you're not tooting your own horn all the time!
- **Use Hootsuite or something similar.** Programs such as HootSuite and TweetDeck will allow you better manage your social media efforts. You

can track several things on one screen, and even schedule tweets ahead of time, so you don't actually have to be in front of the screen to share information. Just be sure you're actively communicating with people who respond to your tweets

ADVANTAGES OF TWITTER

- Using Twitter for marketing means you're able to contact your brand's biggest advocates directly, and they're able to contact you.
- Twitter is direct, compact, and simple to use: The hard 140 character limit means you have to be concise. It's helpful to staying on message and forces you to think clearly before posting something.

- Tweets are designed to spread quickly and easily, and there are multiple options. Tweets can be made a user's favorite, or can be "retweeted" which posts your content directly in their timeline. It's very easy for content to go viral if you attract the right amount of attention, making Twitter marketing fast and effective.
- Hashtags offer simple indexing of content, making marketing on Twitter quick and concise. If you click on a hashtag, you'll see every tweet related to it, and the list will be updated in real time. A snapshot of how your campaign is working can be had with a simple click.

- Media such as photos and video are automatically embedded in the tweet, so fans can see the content without leaving the site

DISADVANTAGES OF TWITTER

- The hard character limit can make it difficult to spread links and other information, especially if you're forced to be vague when you describe it. This can make it difficult to share sites with long URLs, and you'll need to factor that into your Twitter marketing strategy.

- Your Twitter feed can be hacked and used to spread misinformation or otherwise damage your brand.

Twitter is seeking to fight this, using methods such as two-factor identification, but it's still a problem you'll need to account for using Twitter for business marketing.

- As a result of the hacking risks, users can be hesitant to click on links without a full address visible, even from brands they trust.

- Using Twitter for business can backfire. Hashtag campaigns can easily be hijacked by anybody from a competitor to activists, and once users decide to have fun at your expense, it can quickly get out of hand. A good example of this is McDonald's, which sponsored a hashtag only to see everyone from disgruntled employees to animal rights activists use it to embarrass the company. This can also draw negative media attention.

- If the wrong employee is put in charge of the Twitter feed, it can lead to a PR mess, whether it's a problem with an angry customer that gets out of hand or a very public expression of personal opinion. And as the Red Cross found out, there's the potential for very human mistakes. You'll need to weigh this risk in your Twitter marketing plan.

2. FACEBOOK

Facebook was created in 2004, initially it was open to only college students, but it is now available for anyone's use. People can create profiles and connect with friends. Businesses can also make use of it to create pages to connect with their customers and advertise their products and services online.

Almost everyone you relate with are on Facebook which means that they are your potential buyers. Facebook itself has embraced the fact that their social media platform can and will be used as a critical resource for social media marketing. The opportunities are limitless.

BENEFITS OF USING FACEBOOK FOR SOCIAL MEDIA MARKETING

CONNECTING AND BUILDING RELATIONSHIPS

Facebook offers both a live chat and a private message platform that can be used to connect with clients, colleagues, and prospects. Savvy Internet markets will use this feature to create and nurture relationships.

BUILDING BRAND CREDIBILITY

Your business page will allow you to share as much information as you want. Logos and pictures can be used to fortify brand awareness. You also can use the page to share your core brand message with fans, and by interacting with fans, you're sharing your message with all their friends and followers as well.

How to Set Up Your Fan Page On Facebook

While you likely already have a Facebook account for personal use, using a real profile for business and promotion is against the Facebook terms and conditions, so it is important that you create a fan page for your product/service.

1. Visit Facebook.com/page

2. Select your category from the list of options:

a. Local Business or Place

b. Company, Organization or Institution

c. Brand or Product

d. Artist, Band or Public Figure

e. Entertainment

f. Cause or Community

3. Fill in Information: business name, location, website, date launched/founded, hours of operation, etc.

4. Add Photos

5. Suggest the Page to Your Friends: This is a good way to get a jump on the number of likes you have, to start spreading your message and brand presence.

6. Import Contacts: Import email contacts to suggest your page to people you know who not your Facebook friends are.

7. Start Writing Content: Post status updates, share links, etc. to start engaging your fan base.

When you have enough fans, get a vanity URL so it becomes easier to remember/advertise.

How to get likes on facebook

- **Regularly Post a status update.** Tag your business page in it and ask your friends to like the page, and share it with their friends.
- **Get fans to upload and tag photos.** Encourage your fans to upload and tag photos of themselves with your business page.
- **Offer an incentive.** Whether it's a discount on your products or services, or a free eBook/report related to your industry, people will be more likely to

"like" your page when they get something in return.

- **Install a page badge.** Quick, easy way to link to your Facebook page.
- **Install a Facebook "Like Box" on your website.** This enables website visitors to become your fan on Facebook without having to visit Facebook itself, or leave your website.
- **Install a "Like" button on your website.** When users click this, your website (or blog posts, or whatever they click) will show up in their stream, advertising you to their friends.
- Connect the page to Twitter. Anything you post to Facebook will post to Twitter, allowing you to convert your Twitter followers into Facebook fans.

- Link to your page as a place of employment. This enables you to link to your page on your personal profile.
- Include your Facebook page URL in your email signature.
- Include your Facebook page URL on your business cards. This is a good way to promote offline.
- Link to your Facebook page when you leave blog comments. This will build backlinks, to help you increase your rank. Plus, when people see the comment, they can click the link and may "like" your page.
- Link to your Facebook page from your profile. It keeps the link visible to your friends who do not "like" your page already.

- Run a "fans only" contest. People will become fans just to get in on the contest prize.

Advertise your page. Use Facebook advertising to promote your page to people outside your network.

You may run across companies out there promoting fans for purchase. This is typically a practice we shy away from recommending, because the fans are generally fake profiles, and even if they are real people, they are not likely to be targeted customers. You're much better off with a smaller fan base that's more likely to listen to you or make a purchase from you, than you are a higher fan base that doesn't convert to sales for you. Use this tactic at your own risk.

Facebook Advertising

Much like a Google Ad campaign, Facebook has a platform that allows you to pay for ads based on impressions (the number of times they are served) or clicks (the number of times the ad is clicked.) Using Facebook's ad platform, you can super target your ads based on any number of demographics, including: age, location, gender, marital status, interests, etc.

You can set a budget, and when you reach that budget, stop running the ad. The ads are served either on the sidebar of the page, or could be used as a sponsored story. You will have to bid on cost per click, so the lower your bid, the less likely your ad is to be served. The first time you run an ad, it will be approved by Facebook before going live.

Announcing important events Using your Facebook page, you can announce events, such as conferences, appearances, schedules, product launches, discounts, and other special promotion. Fans can recommend the event to friends, to help spread your message further.

3. GOOGLE +

Google+ is ideal for content sharing. It is compatible with youtube. The google hangouts function, circles and communities all make brand awareness and content marketing simple.

Google+ is an individual friendly platform. The communities function works wellto give businesses from all sectors a place to find like-minded individuals and businesses. If you are interested in learning more about your field, then google+ is a place you can do that.

What businesses should be on Google+?

Tech and engineering companies as well as marketing individuals. The top three brands on Google+ are Android, Mashable and Chrome, with Android leading the pack by a significant margin. Below are few facts to know about google +

- Google+ users are 67% male

- The majority are in technical and engineering fields.
- The average age, somewhat surprisingly, is 28.

Although the platform boasts 540 million users, only 300 million or so are active (the huge number of users can be put down, in large, part, to Google's purchase of YouTube in 2006).

4. Pinterest

Pinterest's demographics are interesting not just because it's so astoundingly female-dominated, Pinterest also has the second-highest percentage of internet users in the

50,000+/year income bracket, and 34% of Pinterest users have a household income of 100,00+. Below are few facts about pinterest

- Pinterest has, in the past year, vaulted its way to the #3 spot as most popular social media platform

- 21% of all US adults using it.

- 84% of those users are female - which makes it the second most popular site by far for this demographic.

In fact, Pinterest has far and away the best ROI for those businesses that fit its demographic base. 70% of Pinterest users use the platform to get inspiration on what to buy (compared to, for instance, 17% on

Facebook). So, if your business fits - your business should most definitely sit.

A report from Piqora in November found that the average Pin has a real-world value of 78 cents - making it by far the most valuable social media action that users can take.

The same report found that each pin drove, on average, two website visits and six pageviews. This is especially interesting given that last year jewelry retailer Boticca found that Pinterest traffic to their website spent, on average, more than twice as much as traffic from Facebook ($180 vs $85). And Sephora went further, saying Pinterest users spent 15x as much as Facebook users.

Pinterest is perfect for ecommerce businesses, as not only is a pin worth more than any other social endorsement, they stay influential for a substantially longer period of time. This is because, with Pinterest, users simply keep scrolling down their search results (as the page is never ending)

Which businesses should be on Pinterest?

Fashion, photographers, jewellers, home-hardware stores (DIY). The female-dominated, image-dominated facts of Pinterest make it easy for those brands which naturally lend-themselves in that direction, and very difficult for those brands which don't

5. Instagram

The most important factor for Instagram marketers are the age demographics. Although only 17% of US adults are on the site, a full 43% of mobile owners aged 18-29 are on the site.

- Coming up fast on Twitter is Instagram, with 17% of US adults on the site.

- Interestingly with Instagram, though it's the fifth-most-popular social media platform, it has the second-most devoted users.

- Instagram is the only platform that is actually skewed towards blacks and Hispanics

- 57% of users access the site on a daily basis, only 6 points behind Facebook, and 11% ahead of third-place Twitter.

Which businesses should be on Instagram?

Image-friendly businesses like restaurants, clothes and fashion, food, architecture, technology, designers, etc.

Because of the dominance of the 18-29 age group on Instagram, businesses with that target market should also be on the site

Remember that Instagram users are all amateur-photographers, so you can't just snap an image of your newest dessert and expect it to go viral. Put time and energy into your images and you'll get far better engagement than otherwise.

If you're struggling for content for your Instagram profile, just think about making your business look awesome. Show the fun stuff you're doing, how exciting and innovative your office is. Also pay close attention to current events and holidays, as Instagram (like Twitter) is closely involved in what's trending.

6.LinkedIn

Only 13% of LinkedIn users are signing in daily. People use the platform to check up on business partners, find jobs, and occasionally network - things they do periodically, rather than on a hourly basis like hardcore users of Twitter, Instagram and Facebook.

It is this, despite holding the #2 spot as world's most popular social media platform, that makes LinkedIn notoriously difficult to find success with for businesses. Below are a few facts about Instagram

- The platform touts itself as the 'professional social network', and in that respect it's accurate.

- 38% of internet users with an income of more than $75k are on the platform.

- 79% of LinkedIn users are aged 35 or older, making it the oldest platform in this list.

- 27% of employed Americans are using the platform as well.

- The three dominant sectors on the platform are high tech (14.3%), finance (12.4%) and manufacturing (10.1%). Worth noting is that the legal sector makes up a meager 1.4% of users.

LinkedIn is increasingly losing the business networking battle to Google+, whose Community tool is, somewhat inexplicably, winning next to LinkedIn's groups (despite them being very similar in nature).

All this said, most social media experts are convinced that LinkedIn will grow and thrive

What did he mean? Well, LinkedIn doesn't have the same 'fun' factor that many of the other platforms have. It's not about spending an hour scrolling through your ex-girlfriend's pictures from South East Asia, or about adding a filter to your New Year's pictures, or chiming in on the latest development between Kim Kardashian and... (I don't even know, Justin Bieber?).

LinkedIn is for professionals, and it's about professionals. It's hugely influential in the job hunt, both for employers and applicants. It's great for networking, and the content sharing function is getting better on a weekly basis.

However, is it a revenue-generating platform like Pinterest and Instagram or a brand awareness increase-er like Facebook and Twitter? I'd say no. But feel free to convince me!

Which businesses should be on LinkedIn?
All professionals should be on LinkedIn, as individuals. I also recommend all professional

businesses to be on LinkedIn, though the effort you need to maintain your presence there is significantly less than other platforms. Check in periodically to ensure your profile is stable - but focus your valuable time and energy on the more revenue-generating or awareness-increasing platforms.

There is room for some small businesses to start a conversation or become a trusted source of information with the groups function. I'd recommend all free-lance marketers, bloggers, journalists, designers, etc., to have a significant presence on LinkedIn.

CHAPTER THREE
HOW TO CREATE SOCIAL MEDIA CAMPAIGN THAT WORK

HOW TO CREATE SOCIAL MEDIA CAMPAIGN THAT WORK

People all over the globe connect through social media and indeed we can call this a magnificent technological revolution. Connection with other people on a personal note and for a business purpose is now easier than it ever was. The internet has now turned into a vast marketplace and social media plays an important part in it. If you wish to have a successful social media campaign that is not only solid in theory but one that actually works, then you definitely have to check out the 5 tips discussed below:

Select the right platform
Choosing the correct platform for your niche is far more important than opting for the best one in the market right now. This means that if Facebook is in, it does not automatically mean that it is the right one for your business. You can choose from a wide selection of social media sites namely Twitter, Pinterest, Facebook, Youtube and smaller niche social networks. There are several other new sites that are emerging as of the moment. Take the time to find the right platform for your company and consider even the newer and smaller ones. Once you have figured this out, choose a small target audience for your campaign and start from there.

Analytical Tools Are Vital
You should always monitor how your campaigns are doing. With the help of analytical tools, you'll get to keep track of your posts, images or videos and see how they are performing. You can even check which ones are being shared to others the most. Several third party programs will help you do this and using some of the best ones will help you monitor your efforts especially if you are launching several social media campaigns at once.

Post Frequently
It is very important to know how often and when you should post. If your target market are those who are online during peak hours, then you should post during those times. If your target market includes those who go online during off peak hours then posting your campaigns within that duration is essential.

Post Quality Content
Another vital aspect that you must not overlook is the content of your posts. Text can be very boring and the fact that consumers these days prefer images means that incorporating images along with texts can serve your campaigns better. You may even use videos as people, in most cases, prefer to watch instead of read a full block of text.

CHAPTER FOUR
BENEFITS OF ADDING VISUAL CONTENTS TO YOUR CAMPAIGNS ON SOCIAL MEDIA

BENEFITS OF ADDING VISUAL CONTENTS TO YOUR CAMPAIGNS ON SOCIAL MEDIA

When it comes to marketing content, the web is cluttered and competition is very high. Luckily a great way to make your social media campaign stand out online is to make it more visual. Visual contents are not only easier and faster for the human brain to process, but also is a great way to attract more viewers, clicks and conversions.

Below are some interesting reasons why you should integrate visual content into your campaigns.

1. Visual contents helps to grab the attention of targeted audience. This is why your content must be of a very high quality, very attractive and something that is easily memorable in order for you to be able to break through and capture the attention of your target audience.

2. Visual contents are usually processed faster by the human brain. The human brain can only process a very limited amount of information at any given time. Data that can be processed much faster takes precedence over those that cannot be processed fast when it comes to seizing people's attention.

3. Visual content makes up 93 % of all human communication which is practically non-verbal likewise 90 % of information that enters the brain is practically non-verbal

4. It generates more viewers for your contents and helps your platforms to gain new subscribers and followers

5. Visual contents have the capacity to influence the emotions of humans, they are more understandable and easy to relate with. Targeted audience can better understand your brand's message when you add detailed images and videos to your content.

6. Visual contents that go viral usually bring tons of inbound links to your website especially if people like the content enough to like, share, retweet and comment on it.

7. Visual contents solicits targeted user action much more effectively and gets them to respond quickly than other plain and text-based contents

6 Mistakes in Your Visual Content Strategy to Avoid and Tools to Fix Them

Your team may include a very good and talented graphic designer and highly skilled digital strategists, crafting and sharing visual content on social media is an entirely different ball game

Do you know that when done right, visual content has more than enough potential to be ignore. According to a 2013 Buffer study, Posts with images get 18% more clicks, 89% more likes and 150% more retweets on twitter alone.

Below are mistakes you may likely make or have been making while crafting visual contents and tools to help you correct them.

1. *Posting Similar Images too frequently*

Images with inspirational quotes may earn a click from a few followers, but your visual content strategy is limited if it is based on continuously sharing the same kinds of pictures.

To increase engagement, these visuals should be added to your content:

- **Screenshots:** Educational pictures of your product or service in action, like this one:

- **Infographics:** Visualizations of data or other helpful information – typically long, but can be short and to-the-point for social

- **Preview Images:** Graphics that give a sneak peek at news, events or content

- **Comic Strips:** Cartoons, whether funny or informative, that support your messaging

- **Photography:** Photos that add life to visual content strategies filled with graphics – can be stock or original

- **Memes:** Popular image macros edited to bolster your post or reflect your brand – can certainly give your follower's laugh

- **GIFs:** Looping clips that are funny and relevant to earn likes and shares

- **Video Clips:** Videos from YouTube, Periscope and other platforms embedded in your posts

The Tool to use in achieving these is called Canva

This online image creation suite makes design easy with its intuitive interface. It gives you a library of layouts, illustrations, grids and photographs to play with.

2. Going Overboard with Color

A design with too much white space can look bare, but a busy colour palette creates its own problems. That's because using too many bold tones makes images feel cluttered, and pairing oversaturated hues strains the eyes

To avoid visual content that confuses your audience, stick to two or three colours and tints. Set on a neutral background tone, your choices should have enough contrast to pop and separate from each other.

The tool to use is called Paletton

Drag Paletton's colour wheel cursor to create one-, three- or four-tone schemes.

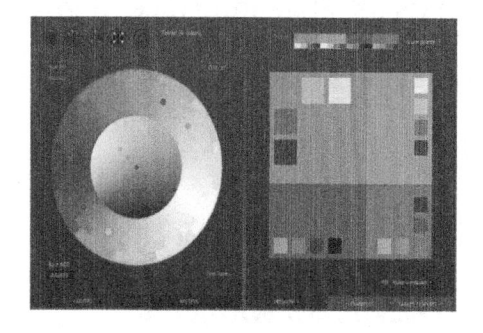

A palette will update on the right of your screen, giving you a look at how well your main color matches with the opposing or complementary ones. Just click on a box to see its RGB code, and design away in your image editor of choice

3. Ignoring Your Website

Updating the visual content on your website should play a role in your social media strategy.

That's because brands like yours aren't the largest sharers of images and videos regular users are.

Almost 50% of adult Internet users share visual media they find when browsing websites, according to a 2013 Pew Research Center study. To boot, research from Curalate states 85% of the average brand's Pinterest presence comes from off-board user activity:

By not including high-quality visuals — including headers, screenshots and tutorial images — you're missing a chance for third-party promotion.

The Tool: WordPress

Almost a quarter of the websites you visit run on WordPress, according to the company's data. Along with thousands of themes to choose from, there's a collection of publishing and media management tools to post and optimize visual content. This makes it easier for visitors find and share your photos and videos.

4. *Leaving Out Call To Actions*

Leaving out a call-to-action (CTA) in your copy or image is a common mistake that hinders interaction. Followers often need encouragement to share or comment.

The best CTAs are short and specific. They should also start with verbs (click) or adverbs (quickly), according to research from Dan Zarrella:

Use action words: more verbs, fewer nouns.

After analyzing 200,000 link containing tweets, I found that tweets that contained more adverbs and verbs had higher CTRs than noun and adjective heavy tweets.

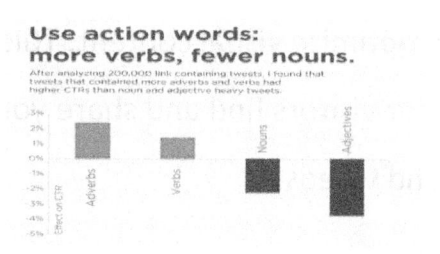

5. *Misrepresenting Your Brand*

You don't have to use a logo to properly represent your brand. In fact, this can sometimes add clutter to your images.

But without it, some social media accounts post content that lacks a clear connection to their products or services. Doing so can leave followers scratching their heads.

Visual content should reflect:

- What your brand stands for

- Your brand's unique or differentiating values

- The topics your audience is interested in

After all, these three factors are probably the reason why fans follow you.

6. *Forgetting to Measure Results*

Don't stay blind to what's working and what's not. Ignoring metrics is the first step in running a social media account that doesn't generate engagement or website traffic.

Based on data, tweak your visual content approach based on:

- Composition

- Posting Time

- CTA

- Hashtag Use

After some testing, you'll discover the best design and posting strategies.

The Tool: Buffer

Buffer is a popular social media scheduling tool, but it also tracks the numbers behind your posts.

For example, it measures the likes, retweets, mentions and clicks each tweet earns. It also tracks *potential* – the number of people who could have viewed a tweet based on who shared it, the hashtags you use and your number of followers. Other tools that can help you measure your performance include

Hootsuite, Feedly, SproutSocial, Google Analytics etc

CHAPTER FIVE
TIPS FROM SOCIAL MEDIA MARKETING GENIUSES

TIPS FROM SOCIAL MEDIA MARKETING GENIUSES

Social media has incredibly become the significant driving force in marketing. But one will normally ask, how does the major companies or brands make the most effective use of this very important tool?

In December, 2014, in a report published by Shareaholic, top 8 social networks drove 31.24% of overall traffic to sites. No wonder more and more people start to understand the vital importance of social media in developing businesses online.

Your potential clients and customers are online across various social media platforms, so if you want to meet and engage them, you have to be where they are. Most importantly, keep in mind that if you still don't use the social media to market your business, your competitors already do.

Here are 20 tips experts in social media marketing have come up with that can help you maximize the effectiveness of social media campaigns

1. Regular posting – The more post you put out there for your audience to see and follow, the more trust you will be able to build over time

2. Deliver relevant content – Always make sure that what your audience hears and sees is interesting and agrees with your brand identity

3. Always make your contents unique – Try to avoid repetition of contents. If you want to stand out on social media platforms, make sure your contents are unique to your brand

4. Share and retweet other people's content - This can be a great way to demonstrate to your audience that you know what is relevant

5. Be as visible as possible – Don't be afraid to follow some of your competitors and even interact with their content

6. Offer help – Endeavour to respond to twitter, Facebook or any other platform whenever you have legitimate answers to questions, and never follow up with calls to action or sales language. Be genuine about wanting to help

7. Learn from your mistakes – Use analytical tools to analyze your past posts to determine what works consistently and what doesn't. Refrain from posting contents that fail to get significant engagement.

8. Always use visual contents on social media contents – Use images and videos to you maximum advantage as they get better engagements than only texts

9. Stop fishing for likes and shares – Try engaging your audience in ways that encourage conversations and interactions. If people find what you post interesting, they will naturally share it.

10. Host live hangouts – This makes the social media experience look more real. Both google hangouts and live twitter events are great tools to use.

11. Make strategic use of hashtags in all social media platforms where they help – Don't just come up with hashtags to add to your post whenever you want to include them in your content. You should thoroughly research trending hashtags. There are times when you can trend but if you want to broaden your reach, you need to follow existing trends.

12. Automate whatever you can – To ensure a fresh flow of content, use automation tools to schedule your posts and keep your content organized.

13. Keep track of what your competitors are posting – Look out for patterns in your competitors' content, and test out similar materials on your own

14. Hold contests and giveaways – Very few things churn up the kind of buzz that is created by giving away freebies, so always consider some friendly competition among your followers

15. Use your email lost to promote your social media content – This can be a great way to drive targeted traffic to your social media platforms

16. Encourage employee engagement on your channels – The people that are working in your organization are your best endorsers. Enlist their help in sharing your content on their individual platforms.

17. Become an authority – Position yourself as a leader in your niche and post contents that proves you as a leader.

18. Take risks - Try something strange or new once in a while and never be afraid to stretch people's perception of your brand

19. Know your audience, listen to them, be useful to them, serve them and invest in them. This usually works in the long run

20. When writing content for your company always ask yourself how your content help your customers

CHAPTER 6
CHARACTERISTICS OF A SUCCESSFUL SOCIAL MEDIA CAMPAIGN

CHARACTERISTICS OF A SUCCESSFUL SOCIAL MEDIA CAMPAIGN

Social media can be a great way of increasing brand awareness, customer engagement and long term loyalty and generating a long term boost in sales, but it's also a potential minefield and in the worst case, a bottomless pit into which you endlessly shovel money with nothing much to show for it. All successful social media campaigns have a few things in common, which every small business owner should be aware of as he or she considers how to maximize their potential on the Internet. With the continuing growth of social media in the marketing world, there is no denying that this medium can be a influential tool for branding a business and interacting with consumers.

TO MAKE CERTAIN YOUR SOCIAL MEDIA CAMPAIGN BECOMES A GREAT SUCCESS, HERE ARE EIGHT CHARACTERISTICS OF EFFECTIVE SOCIAL MEDIA CAMPAIGNS.

What Makes a Successful Social Media Campaign

KNOW YOUR TARGET

Social media campaigns come in different forms and every campaign is distinctive. But what all successful social media campaigns have in common is a clear set of goals and objectives.

You need to take time to think through what you are trying to achieve, the target audience you want to engage without this, your chances of success are going to be slim to zero.

- ❖ Is your main goal to increase brand awareness by reaching out to a new target audience or is it more about educating, informing and engaging existing customers?

- ❖ Is your goal to generate information about a new product launch or event

❖ Is your to increase sales of an underperforming product line?

MAKE USE OF CAPTIVATING VISUALS

Social media campaigns cannot be successful without the use of captivating and attractive visuals. You're going to need first-rate visuals to really grab your target audience attention, posting text and links to articles won't be enough to create a buzz about your brand in the social media market. Not every social media campaign is about generating direct sales and there are plenty of ways to run other types of successful social media campaigns using visuals. It's not that text isn't important; it's more about giving a face to your company. Your target audience needs to know that your company is run by real people. You can do that by uploading photos of your team or pictures and videos of your company events.

DON'T UNDERESTIMATE THE POWER OF A GREAT CONTENT

if you want your campaign to stand out,having a good content is one of the strategies to use to get the attention of your users. The cornerstone of any effective social media campaign is great content presented in an interesting and engaging way. make yourself the place where customers come for advise.to help yourself do better, put yourself in the customer's
shoes, ask and address questions that you would like answered. It leads to more traffic and is considered as one of the best ways by experts.

Use social media platforms to interact with your target audience:

Regular posting on social media platforms is just not adequate, you need to engage your audience as well. This means answering their questions, posting encouraging comments, and rousing excitement among your followers. Social media platforms can be optimally used to address customer's service issues. Make sure you make it easier for users to find you using appropriate tags, e.t.c.

There are several social media networks. You need to use all the available ones to your advantage. Confining yourself to only one platform like Face book for example, is not a very good idea. You can target and reach out to a wider audience if you use other networking sites such as Twitter, Instagram and Pinterest.

POST FREQUENTLY AT OPTIMAL TIMES

It is very important for you to post regularly. Not once a week, not once a month but on a more consistent basis, for example, every day at a specific time. Use An Appropriate Fan Page Name Or Twitter Handle. Make sure that your fan page on Facebook or handle on twitter is as close to the name of your company as possible. This will prevent any confusion and also make it easier for your audience to search for you. For your campaign to be successful you have to ensure your target audience knows about it. Posting once a week or even two times a week is not enough. Knowing the best time can help you optimize when you post to your social networks. You have to be strategic about when you post and how often you do it. It's up to you to figure out the right time to post – and also how frequently to do so. social media tools like Buffer or Hoot Suite can help you to schedule your posts in advance if you're afraid you won't have time to do it each day.

USE THE RIGHT MEDIUM FOR YOUR MESSAGE

. A great message helps your campaigns stand out from the rest .having a great message isn't enough you also have to communicate it through the right channels. Using the right medium should not be limited to face book, and YouTube You can target and reach out to a wider audience if you use other networking sites such as Twitter, Instagram and Pinterest. there are also various medium but if that's not where your target audience hangs out it isn't going to do you much good. It also pays to remember that people tend to act in a different way on different networks so **think about the manners you want your users to take and match the medium to the message..**

ANALYTIC TOOLS ARE VITAL

You should always monitor how your campaigns are doing. With the help of analytical tools, you'll get to keep track of your posts, images or videos and see how they are performing. You can even check which ones are being shared to others the most. Several third party programs will help you do this and using some of the best ones will help you monitor your efforts especially if you are launching several social media campaigns at once.

INTERGRATE EMAIL MARKETING

Email marketing is directly marketing a commercial message to a group of people using. In its broadest sense, every email sent to a potential or current customer could be considered email marketing. It usually involves using email to send ads, request business, or solicit sales or donations, and is meant to build loyalty, trust, or brand awareness. Email marketing can be done to either sold lists or a current customer database. E mail marketing is one of the best channels for a successful social media campaign. E mail marketing is still one of the most effective places to reach a customer, and you can easily turn a social media graphic into an email graphic. You can either create separate promo codes so that you know how many people responded to your campaign by channel or you can use the same promo code for the entire campaign across both channels.

CHAPTER 7
STRATEGIES FOR ENGAGING THE SOCIAL MEDIA AS A MARKETING TOOL

STRATEGIES FOR ENGAGING THE SOCIAL MEDIA AS A MARKETING TOOL

Social media is one of the most powerful tools in marketing your products. If you use it well, you can create a strong personal connection with your prospective clients. However, marketers often make the mistake of using social media without a clear plan. At best, this is a waste of time. To benefit from social media, you need to build a clear strategy that takes into account what you're trying to achieve, who your customers are and what your competition is doing. Have you ever wondered how experts became "The experts" in social media marketing? If you want to know their secrets, then you will find the information presented below extremely useful.

HAVE CLEAR BUSINESS GOALS AND OBJECTIVES

Every business venture needs to have a goal. You have to ask yourself, why do you want to use social media as your marketing tool? What do you want to achieve? Do you wish to have better recognition? Do you want to improve your branding? Don't start if you still haven't found the answer to these questions.

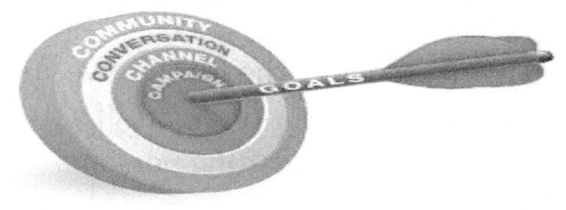

Increase Online Presence in More Social Media Networks

Increasing your presence on various social media platforms is one great strategy of social media marketing, Aside from Facebook and Twitter (another dominant social media force) there are new and upcoming social media networks that are gradually gaining ground in the social market . Among these upcoming social networks, Google+, instagram has gained tremendous ground and has overtook other networks.

Other social networks are also gaining ground, many of which are focusing on graphics, pictures and videos as main focus for content. This includes Pinterest, Vine and Snapchat among others, each focusing on certain user categories and demographics. If you want maximum exposure for your business, it would be wise to develop a strong social media presence not only in Facebook and Twitter but in other social media networks.

Modify Your Content According to Specific Social Media Platform

If you want to attract customers and increase your sales, you need to provide great and high quality content to your audience. The types of content that will inform them of just how useful and relevant your products or services are to them. Highlight its benefits instead of its features when presenting your campaigns or deals and explain why your followers need to buy it. Don't make the error of posting the same content through all the social networks they belong to. By doing so, business fail in delivering the unique user experience social media users are looking for from each particular platform. People who use Pinterest and Instagram often, are more interested in content with visual and will be more attracted to really high-quality pictures and graphics that tell your story. The key to success in this regard is to ensure that your content suit each particular social media platform – and check which format will work best.

ORGANIZE CONTESTS AND PROMOTIONAL ACTIVITIES

One of the most effective strategies for social media in general is to get your targeted audiences directly involved in activities. Conducting contests and other promotional activities are perfect ways for driving their interests and soliciting their participation. You can be as creative as you can be in the type of contests you can conduct, but making use of the sharing and other viral components available in your social network can bring even more exposure for your brand or business as more and more online users join in.

Share more pictures and graphics, and video content

Never underestimates the power of graphics and video content. That's the power of video and other visual elements and learning how to harness the power of these tools and elements can give you maximum exposure for your business. Now, micro-video is slowly gaining ground providing yet another form of content that will change the social media sphere. Snapchat, Twitter's Vine, and the new micro-video sharing feature in Instagram will definitely gain more usage, now that such video sharing activities can be done through smartphones and other Internet-enabled mobile devices

Give out a lot of free trials and deals/discount

A free trial or deal brings the clients in and keeps them there. Giving out discounts off from your regular charges will prove valuable for your targeted clients, the chances of them becoming loyal customers while your business exists can go much higher if you give lots of freebies on a regular basis.

Free deals don't mean giving your main products away. Freebies may be useful articles, free webinars, free videos, and a host of other content that you can give away for free. The more your targeted audiences receive these freebies, the more they can get to know the value of your brand until such time that they transition into paying customers.

BE MORE DETAILED

Attract your targeted audience People love stories and they go to social media networks to read stories, be amazed with interesting features, and learn new things from uploads and shares. To use social media as an effective, you must learn how to tell a story first before you can even sell stuff.

When you tell stories, people will get interested in you and your brand. They would want to know more about you and thus want to read, view or watch more stories, pics and videos about you. There will come a time when their level of interest has grown to the right proportions that they can now be interested in your business, in what you do and in what you sell – and this will be the right time for profits to come rolling in.

REPLY ALL COMMENTS, SUGGESTIONS, AND COMPLAINTS

Social media users comments, suggests, inquire or even complain on business pages and social media profiles. They do this and expect you or your social media manager to give them some form of response or acknowledgement. Social media is "social" and users expect some form of interaction from business owners and digital marketers.

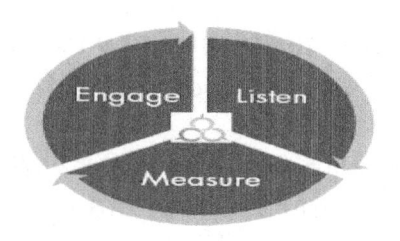

Those who respond to these comments and inquiries will automatically be in a competitive advantage from other businesses or digital marketers who do not. You should also know how to handle or address complaints with proper responses that will satisfy online users. Do not delete these complaints or these users will delete you from their lists. On top of that, always show your gratitude for the time spent by online users in reading, liking, or sharing your posts and content. Doing so will put you in their favor and there will be more than likely chances that they will come back, read more of your content, and even let others know about you and your brand as well.

Made in the USA
Middletown, DE
31 May 2024